Mr. Noisy at the Dude Ranch

Mr. Noisy at the Dude Ranch
© 1999 Creative Teaching Press, Inc.
Written by Margaret Allen, Ph.D.
Illustrated by Kathleen Dunne
Project Director: Luella Connelly
Editor: Joel Kupperstein
Art Director: Tom Cochrane

Published in the United States of America by:
Creative Teaching Press, Inc.
P.O. Box 6017
Cypress, CA 90630-0017

CTP 2916

All rights reserved. No part of this book may be reproduced in any form without the written permission of Creative Teaching Press, Inc.

At sunup, Mr. Noisy left on a trip.
His jeep made lots of noise.

2

"Oh, no!" said Mr. Noisy. "What is that noise?"

3

"Howdy! I am Duke. This is Roy," said Duke.
"Sounds like your jeep needs oil. We can fix it for you.
Join us at Lucky Luke's Dude Ranch."

"A dude ranch sounds like fun!" said Mr. Noisy.
"Yee-hah!" said Duke and Roy. "It is!"

"Howdy!" said Lucky Luke.
"Howdy!" said Mr. Noisy.

6

Lucky Luke gave Mr. Noisy blue jeans.
Jules gave him a rope to use.
June gave him boots and a huge hat.

Yee-hah!

June said, "Oh boy, you are a cute dude now!"
"Yee-hah!" said Mr. Noisy. "I am a cute dude now!"

8

Mr. Noisy had fun at Lucky Luke's Dude Ranch.
He rode Rudy the mule.

He roped the toy bull.

He sang a tune with Duke and Roy.

11

When the jeep had oil, Mr. Noisy left.

He waved to Duke and Roy.
He waved to Lucky Luke and Jules.

He gave the huge hat back to June.

Then Mr. Noisy yelled, "Yee-hah!"

and drove off into the sunset.

BOOK 16: Mr. Noisy at the Dude Ranch

Focus Skills: long u: u-e; /oi/sound: oi, oy

Focus-Skill Words			Sight Word	Story Words	
cute	Luke	noise	when	boots	sunset
dude	Luke's	Noisy		howdy	sunup
Duke	mule	oil		Lucky	waved
huge	tune	boy		ranch	yee-hah
Jules	use	Roy		roped	yelled
June	join	toy		Rudy	

Focus-Skill Words contain a new skill or sound introduced in this book.

Sight Words are among the most common words encountered in the English language (appearing in this book for the first time in the series).

Story Words appear for the first time in this book and are included to add flavor and interest to the story. They may or may not be decodable.

Interactive Reading Idea

Have your young reader reread the book and find and copy on small self-adhesive notes or paper squares all words with the long u (/oo/) sound. Help him or her write phrases or sentences using these words.